This training supplement contains some highlights from the book, *Bridges Out of Poverty: Strategies for Professionals and Communities* and for best results is intended to accompany a Bridges Out of Poverty training workshop.

Bridges Out of Poverty

Strategies for Professionals and Communities

Training Supplement

Ruby K. Payne, Philip DeVol, and Terie Dreussi-Smith
 Bridges Out of Poverty: Strategies for Professionals and Communities Training Supplement
 104 pp.
 Bibliography 95–96
 ISBN: 978-1-938248-74-0
 Excerpts from *Bridges Out of Poverty: Strategies for Professionals and Communities; Getting Ahead in a Just-Gettin'-By World: Building Your Resources for a Better Life; A Framework for Understanding Poverty*

 1. Education   2. Sociology   3. Title

Book design by Paula Nicolella
Cover design by ArtLink, Inc.

Bridges Out of Poverty

Strategies for Professionals and Communities

Training Supplement

Ruby K. Payne
Philip E. DeVol
Terie Dreussi-Smith

Table of Contents

Introduction

How to make the best use of the *Bridges Training Supplement*

Welcome to the Bridges Out of Poverty training.

This supplement to the Bridges training is designed to enhance your learning by highlighting mental models and core concepts that make our approach to poverty unique.

If you are attracted to this work and begin to apply and own it at a personal level, you will find that it deepens your perspective and your work. As you move across the five stages of skill development from novice to expert, you will find that you have lots more to learn and eventually a lot more to share with others.

Having this supplement on your shelf will put the key concepts at your fingertips as you begin to apply Bridges strategies. This, however, cannot replace the books upon which the training is based. We suggest you read *Bridges Out of Poverty* and *Bridges to Sustainable Communities* for a thorough understanding of the material. The supplement does not include every slide the presenter uses; there are simply too many for that to be feasible. The white space on these pages leaves room for your notes and ideas on how you might use the concepts at a personal level, in your organization, and/or in your community.

Since 1999, when *Bridges Out of Poverty* was first published, learning communities have formed in many organizations and communities. Depending on your interests, the areas to expand learning might include engaging people in poverty in the work of building better communities. Or you might explore how to use Bridges concepts in your discipline or sector. Bridges is being used in early-childhood development, education, healthcare, housing, reentry, faith communities, and the workplace.

Bridges has grown into a movement that generates new strategies and solutions that are locally based and community-specific. Happily, many of these innovations have been adapted in many Bridges sites and have spread across the U.S. and in six other countries.

The Bridges learning community now includes an annual conference, regular webinars on many topics, phone conferences for practitioners, and, of course, social media. In addition, practitioners are invited to submit articles for the *From Vision to Action* book series. These peer-selected compendiums describe the innovations and best practices of people like yourself and can be found on our website

By attending this workshop you become eligible to become a Certified Bridges Trainer for your institution. Experience shows that Certified Trainers are necessary to carry the message to more people in your institution and in Bridges Communities. They also help deepen the work, as institutions begin to apply the concepts, redesign programs, and make changes in procedures and policies.

aha! Process offers additional strategies

The explosion in learning that occurs in a number of Bridges sites is captured and shared through the aha! Process website, Facebook page, and newsletters. In addition, many Bridges sites have their own websites and newsletters. aha! Process has published several books and offers trainers and consultants to support the implementation of Bridges concepts.

Enjoy the Bridges workshop! Thanks for all that you are doing to make your community a place where everyone can live well.

Philip E. DeVol

Viewing Economic Class Issues Through the "Triple Lens"

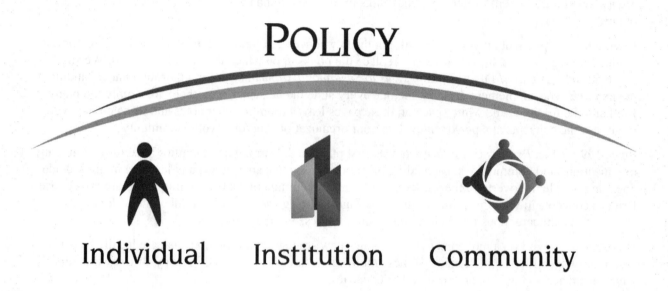

POLICY

Individual   Institution   Community

Copyright J. Pfarr Consulting

Module One
Mental Models

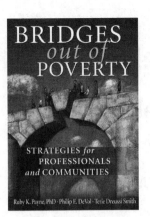

OBJECTIVES

- Explore the concrete experience of people in generational poverty.

- Create a mental model of poverty.

- Analyze elements of the model.

- Create a mental model of middle class.

- Understand the interlocking nature of the models and the demands of the environment.

Mental Models ...

- Are an internal picture of how the world works

- Exist below awareness

- Are theories-in-use, often unexamined

- Determine how we act

- Can help or interfere with learning

For a dialogue to occur we must suspend our mental models.

Notes

No significant learning occurs without a significant relationship.

–Dr. James Comer

Mental Model for Poverty:
What It's Like Now

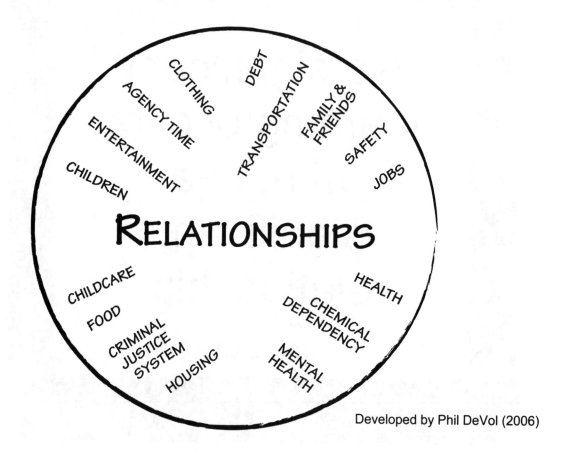

RELATIONSHIPS

CLOTHING

DEBT

AGENCY TIME

TRANSPORTATION

FAMILY & FRIENDS

ENTERTAINMENT

SAFETY

CHILDREN

JOBS

CHILDCARE

HEALTH

FOOD

CHEMICAL DEPENDENCY

CRIMINAL JUSTICE SYSTEM

MENTAL HEALTH

HOUSING

Developed by Phil DeVol (2006)

Notes

Bridges Out of Poverty Training Supplement

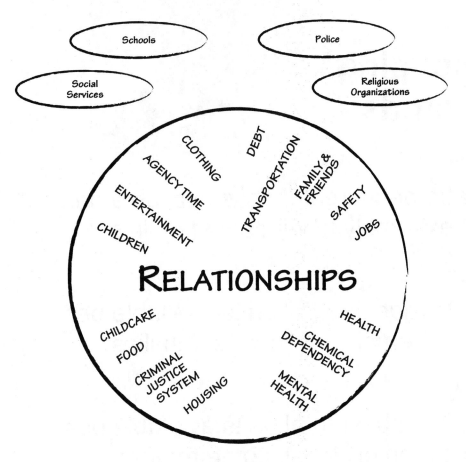

Schools

Police

Social Services

Religious Organizations

RELATIONSHIPS

CLOTHING
DEBT
AGENCY TIME
TRANSPORTATION
ENTERTAINMENT
FAMILY & FRIENDS
CHILDREN
SAFETY
JOBS
CHILDCARE
HEALTH
FOOD
CHEMICAL DEPENDENCY
CRIMINAL JUSTICE SYSTEM
HOUSING
MENTAL HEALTH

Businesses

- Pawn shop
- Liquor store
- Corner store
- Rent to own
- Laundromat

- Fast food
- Check cashing
- Temp services
- Used-car lots
- Dollar store

Notes

stability

time horizon

problem solving

Housing Trends

1991

47 affordable rental units available per 100 extremely low-income families

1997

36 affordable rental units available per 100 extremely low-income families

2015

39 affordable rental units available per 100 extremely low-income renters

Sources: United States Department of Housing and Urban Development, "Rental Housing Assistance—The Worsening Crisis: A Report to Congress on Worst Case Housing Needs" and "Worst Case Housing Needs: 2015 Report to Congress."

Notes ———————————————————————————————————

Affordable Housing: The Growing Gap

The American Community Survey

- In 2010, there were 56 units for every 100 extremely low income families.

- In 2011, there were 5.6 million rental units affordable for the 10.1 million extremely low income renters.

- In 2012 there were 10.1 extremely low income renters producing an absolute shortage of 4.6 million affordable units. There was only an increase of 300,000 affordable units.

- In 2011, 55 units for every 100 extremely low income families without spending more than 30% of their income on housing and utility costs.

Source: United States Census Bureau, "American Community Survey."

Note: The American Community Survey only includes households who are housed, leaving out many people who are homeless.

Notes

Housing stable   30% - 35%

self-sufficiency # income - 74K family of 4

"Housing is the engine that drives the chaos of poverty."

–Paulo Freire

According to "The 2012 Point-in-Time Estimates of Homelessness," there were 243,627 unsheltered homeless people on a single night in 2012. In order to end homelessness, it is critical that communities create and preserve housing that is both affordable and available to those with the lowest incomes.

Source: United States Department of Housing and Urban Development, "The 2012 Point-in-Time Estimates of Homelessness: Volume I of the 2012 Annual Homelessness Assessment Report."

Notes ———————————————————————————————

If you did **everything** your caseworker told you to do—got a job and kept it for a year, never missing a day of work—*how much closer (if at all) would you be to being out of poverty at the end of that year than you were at the beginning?*

Notes

Co-Investigating Health Issues

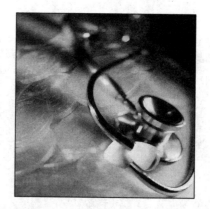

- The SES (socioeconomic status) Gradient

- The richer you are the healthier you are.

- The poorer you are the sicker you are.

- Living in poverty is a risk factor for stress-related illnesses.

- It is NOT entirely due to lack of access.

Source: Robert Sapolsky, *Why Zebras Don't Get Ulcers.*

It's Due to Social Coherence

"Does a person have a sense of being linked to the mainstream of society, of being in the dominant subculture, of being in accord with society's values?"

"Can a person perceive society's messages as information, rather than as noise? In this regard, the poor education that typically accompanies poverty biases toward the latter."

"... has a person been able to develop an ideal set of coping responses for dealing with society's challenges?"

"... does a person have the resources to carry out plans?"

"... does a person get meaningful feedback from society—do their messages make a difference?"

–Robert Sapolsky, Aaron Antonovsky

Notes

Mental Model for
Middle Class

Developed by Phil DeVol (2006)

worry - planning for future

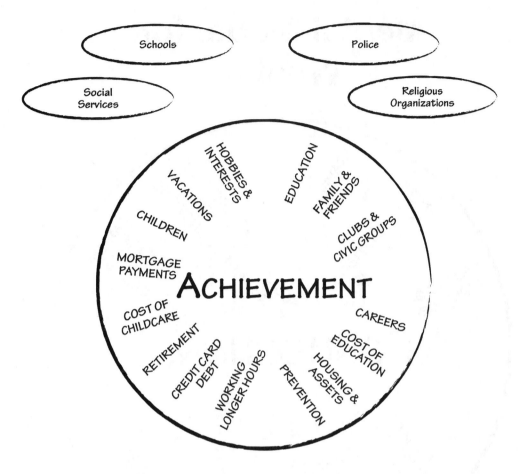

Schools

Police

Social
Services

Religious
Organizations

HOBBIES &
INTERESTS

VACATIONS

EDUCATION

FAMILY &
FRIENDS

CHILDREN

CLUBS &
CIVIC GROUPS

MORTGAGE
PAYMENTS

ACHIEVEMENT

COST OF
CHILDCARE

CAREERS

RETIREMENT

COST OF
EDUCATION

CREDIT CARD
DEBT

HOUSING &
ASSETS

WORKING
LONGER HOURS

PREVENTION

Businesses

- Shopping/strip malls
- Bookstores
- Banks
- Fitness centers
- Vet clinics

- Office complexes
- Coffee shops
- Restaurants/bars
- Golf courses

Notes

Mental Model for Wealth

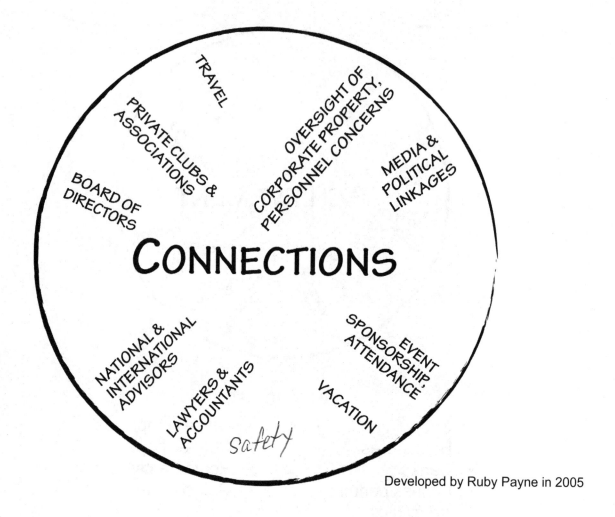

Developed by Ruby Payne in 2005

Bridges Out of Poverty Training Supplement

Tyranny of the Moment

"The need to act overwhelms any willingness people have to learn."

Source: Peter Schwartz, *The Art of the Long View*

"The healthier you are psychologically, or the less you may seem to need to change, the more you can change."

Source: Richard Farson, *Management of the Absurd*

Notes

Mental Model of Generational Poverty

- It is a description of the concrete experience.

- It is an abstract representation of poverty.

- It depicts vulnerability.

- It depicts the relative importance and interlocking nature of the elements.

- It is a depiction of the trap: no future story, no choice, no power.

Notes

poverty- using reactive skills

Module Two Research Continuum

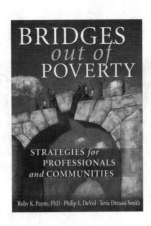

OBJECTIVES

- Understand the many causes of poverty in order to assist people in poverty to build resources.

- Understand what is needed to build sustainable communities.

Poverty Research Continuum

INDIVIDUAL BEHAVIORS AND CIRCUMSTANCES	COMMUNITY CONDITIONS	EXPLOITATION	POLITICAL/ECONOMIC STRUCTURES
Definition: Research on the choices, behaviors, and circumstances of people in poverty	*Definition:* Research on resources and human and social capital in the city or county	*Definition:* Research on the impact of exploitation on individuals and communities	*Definition:* Research on political, economic, and social policies and systems at the organizational, city/county, state, national, and international levels
Sample topics: ~ Racism ~ Discrimination by age, gender, disability, race, sexual identity ~ Bad loans ~ Credit-card debt ~ Lack of savings ~ Skill sets ~ Dropping out ~ Lack of education ~ Alcoholism ~ Disabilities ~ Job loss ~ Teen pregnancies ~ Early language experience ~ Child-rearing strategies ~ Bankruptcy due to health problems ~ Street crime ~ White-collar crime ~ Dependency ~ Work ethic ~ Lack of organizational skills ~ Lack of amenities	*Sample topics:* ~ Racism ~ Discrimination by age, gender, disability, race, sexual identity ~ Layoffs ~ Middle-class flight ~ Plant closings ~ Underfunded schools ~ Weak safety net ~ Criminalizing poverty ~ Employer insurance premiums rising in order to drop companies with record of poor health ~ Charity that leads to dependency ~ High rates of illness leading to high absenteeism and low productivity ~ Brain drain* ~ City and regional planning ~ Mix of employment/wage opportunities ~ Loss of access to high-quality schools, childcare, and preschool ~ Downward pressure on wages	*Sample topics:* ~ Racism ~ Discrimination by age, gender, disability, race, sexual identity ~ Payday lenders ~ Lease/purchase outlets ~ Subprime mortgages ~ Sweatshops ~ Human trafficking* ~ Employment and labor law violations* ~ Wage and benefits theft ~ Some landlords ~ Sex trade ~ Internet scams ~ Drug trade ~ Poverty premium (the poor pay more for goods and services) ~ Day labor	*Sample topics:* ~ Racism ~ Discrimination by age, gender, disability, race, sexual identity ~ Financial oligarchy—the military, industrial, congressional complex ~ Return on political investment* (ROPI) ~ Corporate lobbyists ~ Bursting "bubbles"* ~ Free Trade Agreements ~ Recessions* ~ Lack of wealth-creating mechanisms ~ Stagnant wages* ~ Insecure pensions ~ Healthcare costs ~ Lack of insurance ~ De-industrialization ~ Globalization ~ Increased productivity ~ Minimum wage, living wage, self-sufficient wage ~ Declining middle class ~ Decline in unions ~ Taxation patterns ~ Wealth-creating mechanisms

Source: Philip E. DeVol, *Getting Ahead in a Just-Gettin'-By World.*

Notes _____

how much poverty is generational vs. situational?

Research Continuum Conclusions

- There is valid research in all 4 areas.

- A continuum of strategies covering all 4 areas is needed.

- Ruby Payne's framework offers a way to understand economic issues, to do a critical analysis of poverty and prosperity.

Notes

Community Sustainability Grid
A Comprehensive Planning Tool for Bridges Steering Committees

Name the Barrier: Work one barrier at a time.	Individual Behavior	Human and Social Capital in the Community	Exploitation	Political/ Economic Structures
Individual Action				
Organizational Action				
Community Action				
Policy				

Source: Philip E. DeVol, *Facilitator Notes for Getting Ahead in a Just-Gettin'-By World*.

Module Three Key Points and Bridges Constructs

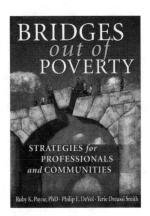

OBJECTIVE

Establish key concepts that underlie *Bridges Out of Poverty* and aha! Process knowedge.

Key Points

1. This workshop focuses on economic environments.

2. Economic class is relative.

3. Economic class is a continuous line, not a clear-cut distinction.

4. Generational poverty and situational poverty are different.

5. This work is based on patterns within the environments of economic class. All patterns have exceptions.

6. An individual brings with him/her the hidden rules of the class in which he/she was raised.

7. Schools and businesses operate from middle class norms and use the hidden rules of middle class.

8. In order to build relationships of mutual respect between economic classes, we need to be aware of more than one set of hidden rules.

9. The more we understand how class affects us and are open to hear how it affects others, the more effective we can be.

10. In order to achieve, one may have to give up relationships (at least for a time).

Bridges Constructs

1. Use the lens of economic class to understand and take responsibility for your own societal experience while being open to the experiences of others.

2. At the intersections of poverty with other social disparities (racial, gender, physical ability, age, etc.), address inequalities in access to resources.

3. Define poverty as the extent to which a person, institution, or community does without resources.

4. Build relationships of mutual respect.

5. Base plans on the premise that people in all classes, sectors, and political persuasions are problem solvers and need to be at the decision making table.

6. Base plans on accurate mental models of poverty, middle class, and wealth.

7. At the individual, institutional, and community/policy levels: Stabilize the environment, remove barriers to transition, and build resources.

8. Address all causes of poverty (four areas of research).

9. Build long-term support for individual, institutional, and community/policy transition.

10. Build economically sustainable communities in which everyone can live well.

Notes _____

Module Four
Hidden Rules

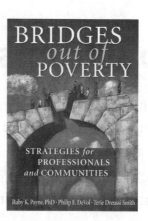

BRIDGES *out of* **POVERTY**

STRATEGIES *for*
PROFESSIONALS
and COMMUNITIES

Ruby K. Payne, PhD · Philip E. DeVol · Terie Dreussi Smith

OBJECTIVE

Understand and give examples of the hidden rules of the 3 economic classes.

Poverty - talks about salary
money becomes communal
food - enough? quantity?
possessions - people/relationships
time - present, survival

Middle - doesn't tell how much earn
like - quality?
possessions - things
time - future

Wealth - don't discuss
food presentation -
possessions - one of a kind, legacies, pedigree
time - legacy, traditions

Bridges Out of Poverty Training Supplement

TIME

POVERTY

Present most important

Decisions made for the moment based on feelings or survival

MIDDLE CLASS

Future most important

Decisions made against future ramifications

WEALTH

Traditions and history most important

Decisions made partially on basis of tradition/decorum

Tools

Future orientation, choice, and power

"If you choose,
then you have chosen."

- What did you do?

- When you did that, what did you want?

- What are 4 other things you could have done instead?

- What will you do next time?

DESTINY

POVERTY

Believes in fate
Cannot do much to mitigate chance

MIDDLE CLASS

free will

Believes in choice
Can change future with good choices now

WEALTH

Noblesse oblige

- give back

DRIVING FORCES

POVERTY

Survival, relationships, entertainment

MIDDLE CLASS

Work, achievement, material security

WEALTH

Financial, political, social connections

Notes ────────────────────────────────────

POWER

POVERTY

Power linked to personal respect
Ability to fight
Can't stop bad things from happening

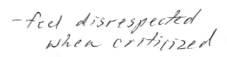

−feel disrespected when critisized

MIDDLE CLASS

Power/respect separated
Responds to position
Power in information and institutions

WEALTH

Power in expertise, connections
Power in stability
Influences policy and direction

Notes ———

Tools

Relationship = power and respect

Relationships are often motivating factors.

Source: J. Pfarr Consulting

Module Five
Language

OBJECTIVES

Distinguish the different registers of language and assist people in developing formal register.

Understand how language register, story structure, and language experience influence cognitive development.

Registers of Language

REGISTER	EXPLANATION
FROZEN	Language that is always the same. For example: Lord's Prayer, wedding vows, etc.
FORMAL	The standard sentence syntax and word choice of work and school. Has complete sentences and specific word choice.
CONSULTATIVE	Formal register when used in conversation. Discourse pattern not quite as direct as formal register.
CASUAL	Language between friends characterized by a 400- to 800-word vocabulary. Word choice general and not specific. Conversation dependent upon non-verbal assists. Sentence syntax often incomplete.
INTIMATE	Language between lovers or twins. Language of sexual harassment.

Adapted from Martin Joos' research by Ruby K. Payne, *A Framework for Understanding Poverty.*

Notes ─────────────────────────────────

Kaplan Discourse

Formal

Casual

Story Structure

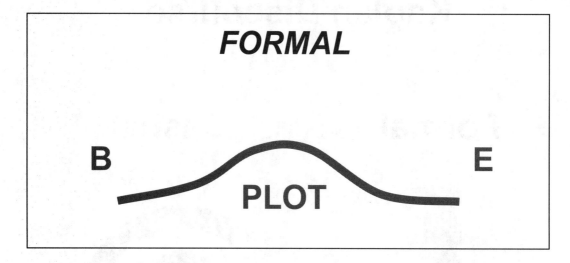

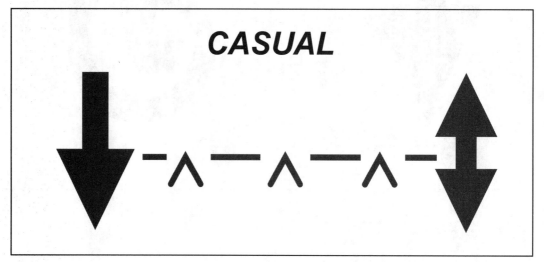

Bridges Out of Poverty Training Supplement

Research about language in children from ages 1 to 4 in stable households by economic group.

Research About Language in Children from Ages 1 to 4 Years from Stable Households by Economic Group			
Number of words exposed to	Economic group	Affirmations	Prohibitions
13 million words	Welfare	1 for every	2
26 million words	Working class	2 for every	1
45 million words	Professional	6 for every	1

Source: Betty Hart and Todd R. Risley, *Meaningful Differences in the Everyday Experience of Young American Children.*

Notes

If an individual depends upon a random episodic story structure for memory pattern, lives in an unpredictable environment, and does not have the ability to plan, then …

The individual **cannot plan.**

If an individual cannot plan, he/she **cannot predict.**

If an individual cannot predict, then he/she **cannot identify cause and effect.**

If an individual cannot identify cause and effect, he/she **cannot identify consequences.**

If an individual cannot identify consequences, he/she **cannot control impulsivity.**

If an individual cannot control impulsivity, he/she **has an inclination to criminal behavior.**

Adapted from the work of Reuven Feuerstein.

Notes

MEDIATION		
Identification of the stimulus	Assignment of meaning	Identification of a strategy

WHAT   WHY   HOW

Adapted from the work of Reuven Feuerstein.

Notes

Voices

<table>
<tr>
<td>Child</td>
<td>

Defensive, victimized, emotional, whining, losing attitude, strongly negative, non-verbal.
- **Quit picking on me.**
- **You made me do it.**
- **I hate you.**

</td>
</tr>
<tr>
<td>Parent</td>
<td>

Authoritative, directive, judgmental, evaluative, win-lose mentality, demanding, punitive, sometimes threatening.
- **You shouldn't do that.**
- **Life's not fair. Get busy.**

</td>
</tr>
<tr>
<td>Adult</td>
<td>

Non-judgmental, free of negative non-verbal, factual, often in question format, attitude of win-win.
- **In what ways able to resolve?**
- **What are choices in this situation?**

</td>
</tr>
</table>

Adapted from work of Eric Berne.

Notes ───

Module Six Family Structure

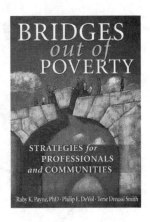

OBJECTIVE

Understand family structure and the resulting behavioral patterns in generational poverty.

Family Structure

Jane

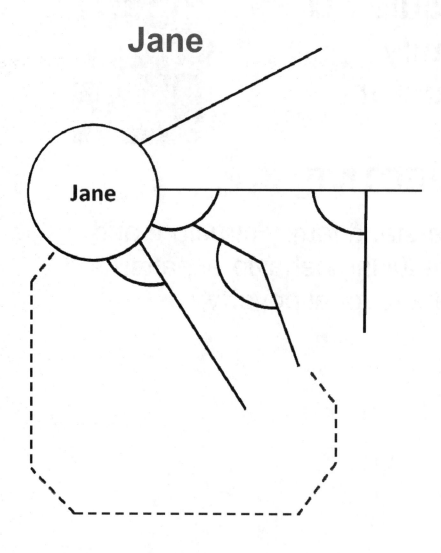

Family Structure

Mary and the Eyebrows

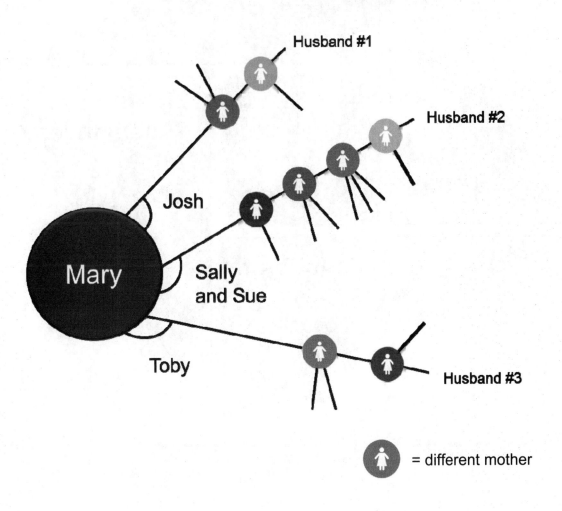

Husband #1

Husband #2

Josh

Mary

Sally
and Sue

Toby

Husband #3

= different mother

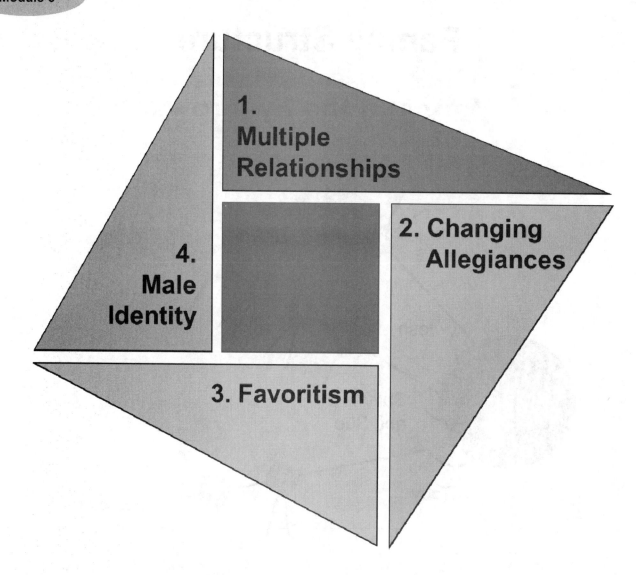

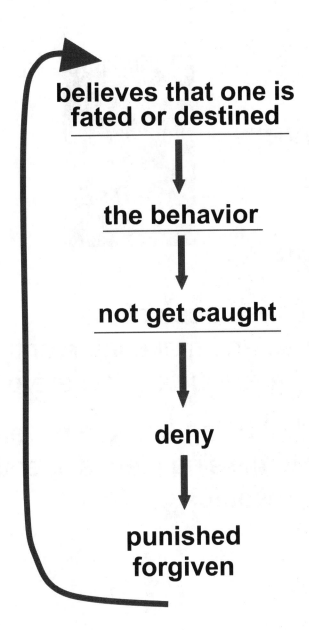

believes that one is
fated or destined

↓

the behavior

↓

not get caught

↓

deny

↓

punished
forgiven

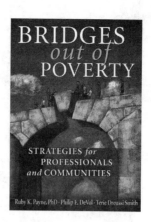

Module Seven
Resources

OBJECTIVES

- Analyze the 8 resources of the client/employee and make interventions based on those resources that are present.

- Understand that being stuck in poverty is often related to missing pieces; identify ways to build resources.

Definition of Poverty

To better understand people from poverty, the definition
of poverty will be
***"the extent to which an individual
does without resources."***

Those resources are the following …

Definition of Resources

FINANCIAL
Being able to purchase the goods and services of that class and sustain it.

EMOTIONAL
Being able to choose and control emotional responses, particularly to negative situations, without engaging in self-destructive behavior. Shows itself through choices.

MENTAL
Having the mental abilities and acquired skills (reading, writing, computing) to deal with daily life.

SPIRITUAL
Believing in (divine) purpose and guidance.

PHYSICAL
Having physical health and mobility.

SUPPORT SYSTEMS
Having friends, family, and backup resources available to access in times of need. These are external resources.

RELATIONSHIPS/ROLE MODELS
Having frequent access to adult(s) who are appropriate, **nurturing,** and who do not engage in destructive behavior.

KNOWLEDGE OF HIDDEN RULES
Knowing the unspoken cues and habits of a group.

Notes

Questions to Ask About Resources

FINANCIAL

Is $574 per month per person available? *

Is there enough income to cover all expenses?

Is your credit/debt ratio above 37%?

Do you spend more than 30% of your income on rent/mortgage?

Do you have enough savings to cover six months of expenses?

* Based on 125% of 2010 Poverty Guidelines for Family of Four: $27,563 per year/$2,297 per month.

EMOTIONAL

Is there evidence that the individual has persistence?

Does the individual have the words to express feelings in a way others can receive?

Does the individual have coping strategies (for adverse situations) that are not destructive to self or others?

MENTAL

Can the individual read, write, and compute?

Can the individual plan?

Can the individual problem-solve?

Can the individual understand cause and effect, then identify consequence?

SPIRITUAL

Does the individual believe in divine guidance and assistance?

Does the individual have belief in something larger than self?

Does the individual perceive an abstract and larger perspective that provides depth and meaning to life (culture, science, higher power, etc.)?

Notes

Questions to Ask About Resources
(continued)

PHYSICAL

Can the individual take care of him-/herself without help?
Does the physical body allow the person to work and to learn?
Does the individual have transportation resources to get from one place to another?
Does the individual have health and wellness?

SUPPORT SYSTEMS AND SOCIAL CAPITAL

Who is the individual's bonding social capital? Is it positive?
Who is the individual's bridging social capital? Is it positive?

KNOWLEDGE OF MIDDLE CLASS HIDDEN RULES

Does this individual know the hidden rules of work and school?
How important are achievement and work?
Will this individual give up relationships for achievement (at least for some period of time)?

Notes ──

All Three Classes Come to the Decision Making Table to Solve Community Problems

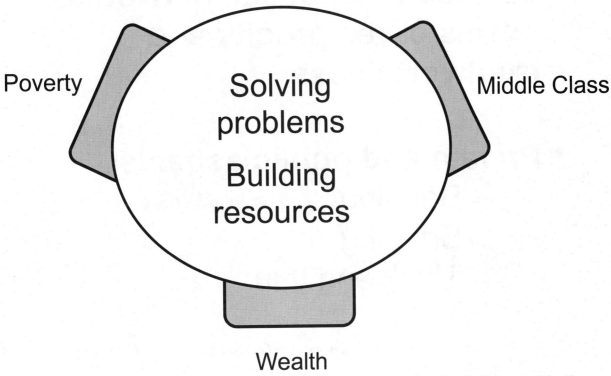

Poverty

Solving
problems

Building
resources

Middle Class

Wealth

Developed by Terie Dreussi-Smith,
Jodi R. Pfarr, and Philip E. DeVol

Notes ———————————————————————

Definition of Social Capital

- **Connections, social networks, norms of reciprocity and trustworthiness**

- **Private and public aspects**
  - Bonding
  - Bridging
  - Thick and thin

Source: Robert D. Putnam, *Bowling Alone: The Collapse and Revival of American Community*.

Mental Model of Social Capital

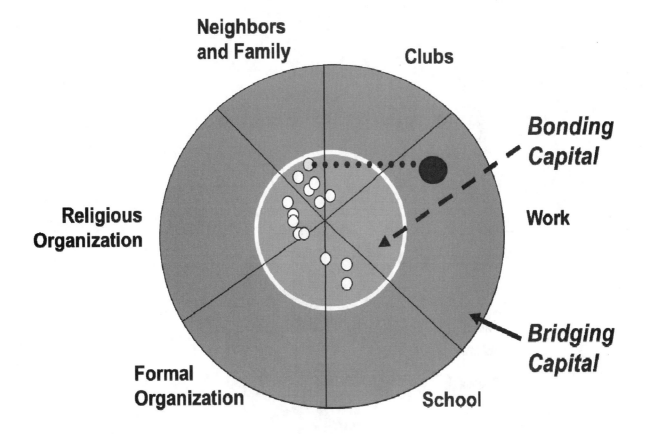

Source: Philip E. DeVol, *Getting Ahead in a Just-Gettin'-By World*.

Mental Model of Resources

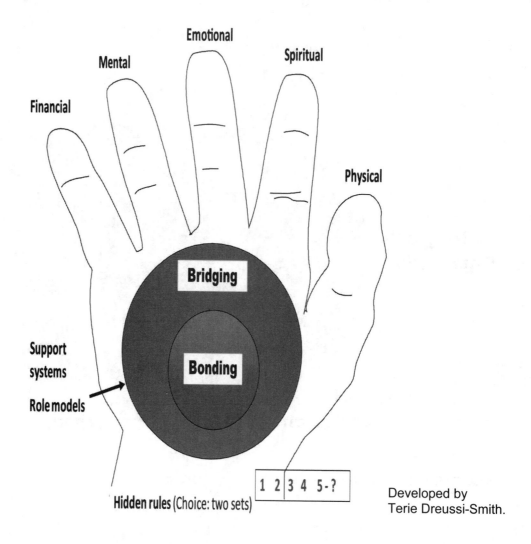

Developed by
Terie Dreussi-Smith.

	Financial	Emotional	Mental	Spiritual	Physical	Support Systems	Relationships/ Role Models	Knowledge of Hidden Rules	Integrity and Trust	Motivation and Persistence	Formal Register
Building											
Bringing											

Reprinted with permission. Copyright J. Pfarr Consulting.

Continuum of Those Who Take Part in Getting Ahead

Extremely Unstable Environments

Unstable Environments

Fairly Stable Environments

Daily life disrupted by violence, illness, addiction, disabilities, and/or unstable community conditions. Highly affected by generational poverty. Stabilizing the environment and building resources may take a very long time.

Daily life can be stabilized enough with supports to attend weekly or bi-weekly workshops. People in generational and situational poverty. Building resources may take a long time.

Daily life can be organized fairly easily. May be able to build resources rather quickly. Some people in situational poverty.

Notes _____

Facilitator Notes for Getting Ahead in a Just-Gettin'-By World, Appendix 1

- **Expectations of a Getting Ahead investigator:**

    - Attend all sessions.

    - Make up any missed work.

    - Create and live by group rules.

    - Be accountable to the group for being on time and completing work he/she agreed to do.

Source: Philip E. DeVol, *Facilitator Notes for Getting Ahead in a Just-Gettin'-By World*.

Notes

Resources Added to *Getting Ahead*

Integrity and trust:

Your word is good, you do what you say you will do, and you are safe.

Motivation and persistence:

You have the energy and drive to prepare for, plan, and complete projects, jobs, and personal changes.

Formal register:

You have the emotional control, vocabulary, language ability, and negotiation skills to succeed in work and/or school settings.

Source: Philip E. DeVol, *Facilitator Notes for Getting Ahead in a Just-Gettin'-By World*.

Notes

Mental Model of Resources

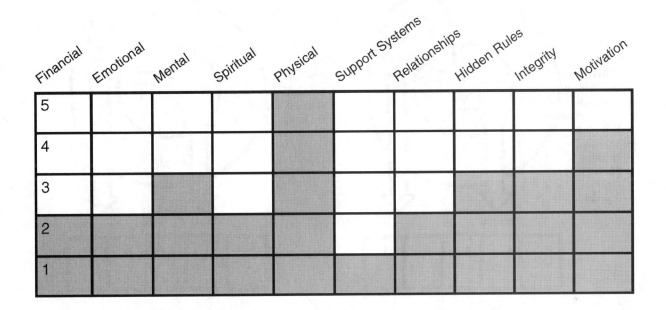

Source: Philip E. DeVol, *Facilitator Notes for Getting Ahead in a Just-Gettin'-By World*.

Notes

- bringing resources
- building resources

Theory of Change for *Getting Ahead*

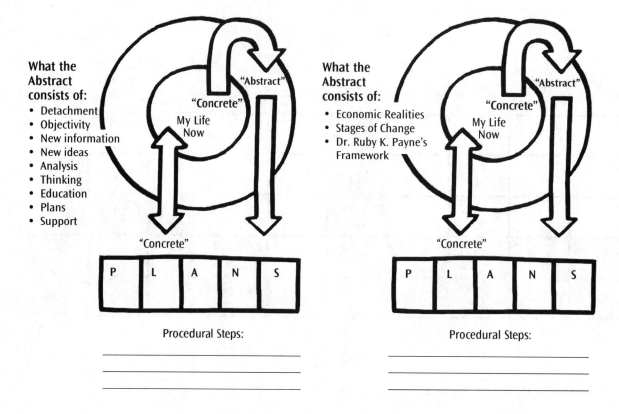

What the Abstract consists of:
- Detachment
- Objectivity
- New information
- New ideas
- Analysis
- Thinking
- Education
- Plans
- Support

"Abstract"

"Concrete"
My Life Now

"Concrete"

P	L	A	N	S

Procedural Steps:
_____
_____
_____

What the Abstract consists of:
- Economic Realities
- Stages of Change
- Dr. Ruby K. Payne's Framework

"Abstract"

"Concrete"
My Life Now

"Concrete"

P	L	A	N	S

Procedural Steps:
_____
_____
_____

Source: Philip E. DeVol, *Facilitator Notes for Getting Ahead in a Just-Gettin'-By World.*

Notes

3 Ways to Move from the Concrete to the Abstract

- Use mental models.

- Make the information meaningful and relevant.

- Design programs that explore the discrepancy between the current behavior and the future story.

Source: Philip E. DeVol, *Facilitator Notes for Getting Ahead in a Just-Gettin'-By World*.

Learning Task

Using the *Bridges* Approach

- Identify a common problem that people who come to your organization face (joblessness, homelessness, seeking food).

- Then fill in the *Bridges* Grid. Start with Individual Action and move across the row filling in ideas for what one might do to solve the problem.

- Then move down to the Agency Action, Community Action, and Policy rows and continue developing strategies.

Notes _____

Processing

- What resources might the person want to build?

- What support can your agency provide?

- What supports might your community provide?

- What policy changes might be needed?

Cascade Engineering

Welfare-to-career employee retention rates
- 1991–June 1999—29%
- December 1999—80%
- Annual retention rate through August 2010—71.5%

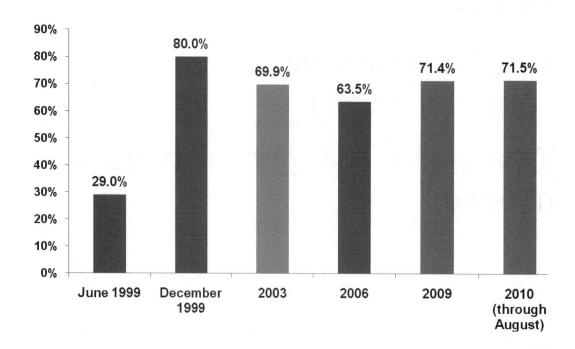

Bridges Out of Poverty Training Supplement

Cascade Engineering

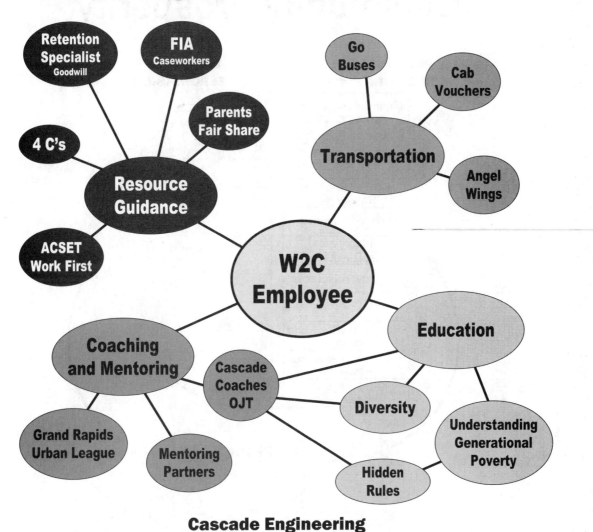

Cascade Engineering

Notes _____

Mental Model for Community Prosperity

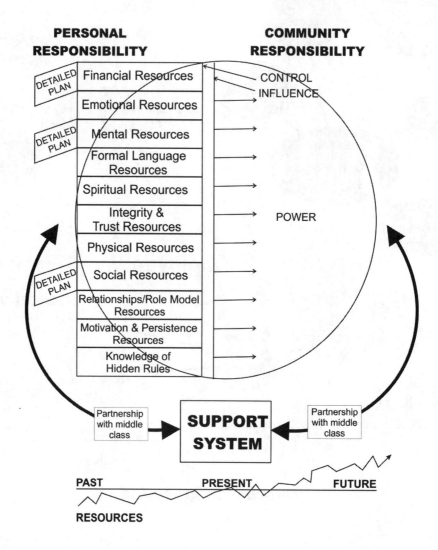

PERSONAL
RESPONSIBILITY

COMMUNITY
RESPONSIBILITY

DETAILED PLAN — Financial Resources

CONTROL

INFLUENCE

Emotional Resources

DETAILED PLAN — Mental Resources

Formal Language Resources

Spiritual Resources

Integrity & Trust Resources

POWER

Physical Resources

Social Resources

DETAILED PLAN — Relationships/Role Model Resources

Motivation & Persistence Resources

Knowledge of Hidden Rules

Partnership with middle class

SUPPORT SYSTEM

Partnership with middle class

PAST   PRESENT   FUTURE

RESOURCES

Notes

Principles of Change

- People in poverty are problem solvers.
- Stabilize the environment.
- Provide support during transition.
- Build future stories, practice choice, and develop power and influence.
- Communities, families, and individuals build resources.
- Bring members of all 3 economic classes to the table.
- Develop strategies across all 4 areas of research.
- Plan, monitor, and evaluate using the Social Health Index.

Notes

STRATEGIES

HIDDEN RULES	RESOURCES
I. Learn the rules of economic class in order to understand clients and employees who come from generational poverty. II. Teach the hidden rules; clients from poverty need to know two sets of hidden rules. III. Share the awareness of hidden rules with community partners. IV. Examine and re-examine your personal mental models about people in poverty to avoid stereotyping clients/employees. V. Use the understanding provided by awareness of hidden rules to counter stereotyping of people in poverty.	I. Examine the eight resources for individuals from poverty to become aware of internal strengths and environmental assets of clients and new hires. II. Build interventions on strengths. Look for the "half full" part of the glass. III. Engage individuals in poverty in solving community problems. IV. Provide economic opportunities for clients. Foster the development of small businesses. V. Create and support micro-credit opportunities. VI. Assist in the development of associations that are largely independent of agencies/institutions. VII. Refer clients to associations that match the individual's interests, skills, talents, and gifts.

FAMILY STRUCTURE	LANGUAGE, STORY STRUCTURE, AND COGNITION
I. Learn the rules of economic class in order to understand clients and employees who come from generational poverty. II. Provide additional support systems through associations, individual contact, and resource enhancement. III. Recognize that change takes time and happens in phases. IV. Provide long-term support and relationships. V. Recognize that some family members will resist change and may impede the efforts of individuals moving out of poverty. VI. Recognize that moving out of poverty may include a grieving process for some individuals. VII. Train front-line staff in the grief process so that they understand the emotional toll on clients and new hires. VIII. Recognize that domestic violence is more prevalent in poverty and that some clients may be at real risk during the change process.	I. Teach formal register to new hires and clients so that they become "bi-lingual." II. Encourage front-line staff to understand casual register. Staff must be able to translate forms and instructions from formal to casual register. III. Rewrite forms to be more meaningful. IV. Reduce middle-class "noise" by using meaningful mental models, drawings, stories, and analogies. V. Work with community partners to promote a rich language experience for children from birth to 3 years of age. VI. Reframe conflicts resulting from the use of casual register into learning experiences.

STRATEGIES

CREATING RELATIONSHIPS	SUPPORT SYSTEMS
I. Seek first to understand. II. Make deposits, not withdrawals. III. Appreciate humor and entertainment. IV. Respect relationships. V. Wait for the invitation. VI. Use the adult voice. VII. Use dialogue and discussion appropriately. VIII. Mediate. IX. Solve concrete problems. X. Be aware of one's own mental models. XI. Communicate without "noise." XII. Identify gifts, talents, and skills. XIII. Respect the importance of freedom of speech and personality. XIV. Think of people in poverty as the solution to problems.	I. Inventory individuals for gifts, talents, and skills. II. Inventory community associations, as well as service providers. III. Plan for long-term relationships. IV. Introduce individuals to others who have been successful and who have common interests. V. Recognize that change is a process, not an event. VI. Develop economic opportunities whenever possible.

MENTAL MODELS	MOTIVATION
I. Drawing, sketching. II. Time. III. Planning backward. IV. Formal register. V. Space. VI. Organizational change process. VII. Change process of each discipline. VIII. Limit situations. IX. Mental models for poverty and prosperity. X. Stories, metaphors, analogies. XI. Dealing with emotional blackmail. XII. Mediation.	I. Design structure. II. Reframe power struggles. III. Metaphor stories. IV. Voices. V. Health realization, psychology of the mind. VI. Managing emotional blackmail. VII. Reframe penance/forgiveness cycle. VIII. Behavioral analysis. IX. Win-win process.

STRATEGIES

CO-EXISTING PROBLEMS	REDESIGN AND CQI (CONTINUOUS QUALITY IMPROVEMENT)
I. Identify barriers. II. Identify strengths. III. Asset development. IV. Capacity enhancement. V. Tucker Signing Strategies. VI. Best practices by discipline.	I. Theory of business. II. Client life cycle. III. Policy and procedure redesign. IV. Staff assignments. V. Orientation. VI. Engaging and inviting parents. VII. Utilizing information. VIII. Support growth of associations. IX. New-science strategies.

COMMUNITY STRATEGIES

I. Inventory of individuals.
II. Inventory of associations.
III. Inventory of service providers.
IV. Inventory of governmental agencies.
V. Identify connectors, mavens, salespeople.
VI. Community client life cycle.
VII. Make messages "sticky."
VIII. Change the context.
IX. Build partnerships with associations.
X. Build partnerships with providers.
XI. Cost benefits of collaboration.
XII. Provide resources as needed.
XIII. Provide economic opportunity.
XIV. Provide micro-credit.

Utilizing the Bridges Out of Poverty Concepts

Name:_____

Organization:_____

What are three ways you can improve your personal skills for working with individuals in poverty?

1.

2.

3.

What are three ways you can improve programming, theory, and structure to better serve individuals in poverty?

1.

2.

3.

What are three ways you can improve the community system to better serve people in poverty?

1.

2.

3.

What, if any, follow-up services does your organization need?

12 Thinking Tools for Bridges Out of Poverty Initiatives

by Philip E. DeVol

Theory and Practice in a Bridges Initiative

Bridges Out of Poverty workshops are known for changing the way people think about poverty and economic class. People have "aha" moments that deepen into insights that are so powerful that there is no going back to their old way of thinking. These in turn deepen into paradigm shifts that alter every aspect of their work on poverty. It is not the purpose of this paper to reiterate the basic content of Bridges but to distinguish between theory and practice in Bridges work. The practices may be varied and complex but the theory must bring clarity to our work.

The theory: When individuals are under-resourced to the extent that they spend most of their time and energy trying to keep their heads above water, their daily living experience becomes dominated by the tyranny of the moment. Rather than spending time and energy building resources for a better future, their time and energy go toward trying to stabilize their unstable world, and they end up staying stuck in a life of poverty.

When institutions and communities are under-resourced to the extent that they spend too much time and energy trying to keep their heads above water, they behave in very similar ways to under-resourced individuals: They spend their time solving concrete problems using strategies that originate from the same mindset that created the problems.

The solution for individuals, institutions, and communities is to build stability and resources.

The practice: Bridges initiatives have a common language about poverty and matters of economic class. Bridges initiatives use the following 12 thinking tools to build stability and resources at four levels: individual, institutional, community, and policy. The goal of Bridges initiatives is to prevent poverty, alleviate suffering, aid those who are making the transition out of poverty, and create communities where everyone can live well.

Anyone familiar with Bridges will be aware of most of the following mental models. Mental models are used to help make abstract ideas more concrete and to help us remember ideas by representing them with visual images. Mental models help us learn quickly, remember longer, and apply the concepts in deeper ways. Thus the term *thinking tools*.

Mental models tend to provide our first "aha" moment and new insights that attract us to Bridges. For some people, attraction moves quickly to action. Early adapters have generated a number of programs and approaches that have become foundational to the Bridges movement. But poverty is a complex problem that demands a comprehensive approach. And therein lies the challenge. Poverty is not resolved with a single program or even set

Excerpted from Revised Edition of *Bridges to Sustainable Communities* by P. E. DeVol (2015). Published by aha! Process, Inc.

of programs, because there so many variables. Bridges is not a program. It is a set of constructs that can be applied in many settings and in many ways.

The ensuing thinking tools can help individuals, organizations, and communities create, embed, and expand solutions.

The pattern for explaining these 12 thinking tools has these six elements:

a. A problem statement describing how things are now
b. A mental model representing the thinking tool
c. The context in which the tool is applied—a description of how it fits into Bridges work
d. Core ideas of the thinking tool
e. Ways to use the tool
f. Information on where to learn more

Table of Contents: 12 Thinking Tools

Excerpted from Revised Edition of *Bridges to Sustainable Communities* by P. E. DeVol (2015). Published by aha! Process, Inc.

1. Triple Lens

How things are now: Individuals learn about poverty through personal experience, stories in the news, reading, and general debate—but rarely through an intention to fully understand this complex problem. Without a structure for processing the complexities of poverty, without a way to organize our thinking, our responses to poverty will continue to be ineffective.

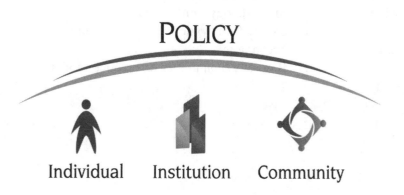

© J. Pfarr Consulting

A woman in poverty saw a sign on a caseworker's door that read, "Your failure to plan does not constitute an emergency for me." The triple lens has us first analyze the dynamics between the client and caseworker, helping to explore and decode class interactions from both sides of the desk. It would deepen the understanding by analyzing the driving forces of the institution and the role of the institution in the community.

By using the triple lens, we develop new ideas, discover how to apply new concepts, and make necessary changes. This tool helps us do thorough work.

As for clients who are late, it's possible that they might need to make some changes, but this tool reminds us that they don't need to change any more than those who are in the institutions and community.

Context: The triple lens is a structure by which poverty can be assessed and processed thoroughly. Looking at poverty through a single lens—be it individual, organizational, or community—will not provide the depth of understanding that comes from viewing poverty through all three lenses.

Core ideas: Poverty elicits strong opinions; it's easy to take sides or to blame the other person or institution. This thinking tool helps replace judgments with understanding. The first place that conflicts usually occur is the interaction between people in poverty and people in institutions, such as caseworkers, supervisors, and healthcare workers.

How to use the tool

- Use the triple lens to deepen understanding of the core elements of a Bridges workshop: the mental models of class, the causes of poverty, hidden rules, resources, and language.

- When embedding the concepts in our organization or designing a new community program, the question becomes: "What would we learn by applying the triple lens?"

Learn more: Read *Tactical Communication: Mastering effective interactions with citizens from diverse economic backgrounds,* Jodi R. Pfarr, 2013.

Excerpted from Revised Edition of *Bridges to Sustainable Communities* by P. E. DeVol (2015). Published by aha! Process, Inc.

74   *Bridges Out of Poverty Training Supplement*

2. Mental Models of Economic Class

How things are now: In the United States few of us know how people in other classes live. Social connectedness has been decreasing since the 1970s as income segregation in housing has separated us into economic enclaves. This has led to a lack of knowledge and understanding between/among the classes. Programs in education, health, and workforce development that are for people in poverty are more often than not designed without their input. Thus the phrase, "If it's *about* us, without us, it's not *for* us."

Context: These three mental models came from the first investigations people in poverty made while Getting Ahead was being created. They were quickly picked up by Bridges trainers and became icons for the understanding we have of class issues. These distinct environments arise when there is great inequality in wealth. The hidden rules arise from these environments and deepen the impact of being raised in generational poverty, generational middle class, and generational wealth.

Mental Model for Poverty   **Mental Model for Middle Class**   **Mental Model for Wealth**

RELATIONSHIPS (with surrounding labels: CLOTHING, DEBT, FAMILY & FRIENDS, AGENCY TIME, TRANSPORTATION, SAFETY, ENTERTAINMENT, JOBS, CHILDREN, HEALTH, CHILDCARE, CHEMICAL DEPENDENCY, FOOD, CRIMINAL JUSTICE SYSTEM, HOUSING, MENTAL HEALTH)

Developed by P. DeVol, 2006

ACHIEVEMENT (with surrounding labels: HOBBIES & INTERESTS, EDUCATION, VACATIONS, FAMILY & FRIENDS, CHILDREN, CLUBS & CIVIC GROUPS, MORTGAGE PAYMENTS, COST OF CHILDCARE, CAREERS, RETIREMENT, COST OF EDUCATION, CREDIT CARD DEBT, HOUSING & ASSETS, WORKING LONGER HOURS, PREVENTION)

CONNECTIONS (with surrounding labels: TRAVEL, PRIVATE CLUBS & ASSOCIATIONS, OVERSIGHT OF CORPORATE PROPERTY, PERSONNEL CONCERNS, BOARD OF DIRECTORS, MEDIA & POLITICAL LINKAGES, NATIONAL & INTERNATIONAL ADVISORS, EVENT SPONSORSHIP ATTENDANCE, LAWYERS & ACCOUNTANTS, VACATION)

Developed by R. Payne, 2005

Analytical Terms	
Mental bandwidth	Concrete/abstract
Power	Invisible, little influence/powerful
Stability	Daily instability/long-term stability
Time horizon	Tyranny of the moment/long view
Problem-solving approach	Reactive problem solving with relationships/proactive problem solving
Financial security	Daily insecurity/long-term security

Source: Philip E. DeVol, adapted from *Facilitator Notes for Getting Ahead in a Just-Gettin'-By World,* 2013.

Excerpted from Revised Edition of *Bridges to Sustainable Communities* by P. E. DeVol (2015). Published by aha! Process, Inc.

Core ideas: The environments represented by the mental models explain differences in such aspects of life as driving forces, stability, power, time for abstract endeavors, time horizon, financial security, and problem-solving approaches. Poverty is experienced locally. Poverty in a Rust Belt city is different from poverty in a rural county or a prosperous, high-tech city; the barriers and opportunities will be specific to the Bridges site.

Poverty is also experienced differently by each individual according to a number of conditions and influences including race, gender, ethnicity, age, disability, sexual orientation, immigrant status, and religion.

How to use the tool

- Learn about poverty in your community by engaging Getting Ahead investigators and graduates. They can share the results of their investigations into poverty as it is experienced locally, their assessment of community, and their mental model of community prosperity.

- Include Getting Ahead graduates as speakers and facilitators during Bridges workshops and events, poverty simulations, and media events. Use knowledge of the environments and hidden rules to navigate new settings more skillfully.

- Use knowledge of the environments and hidden rules to navigate social settings more skillfully.

- During meetings, establish a safe setting and process so people can speak freely about hidden rules that are broken.

- Design programs so that hidden rules that break relationships are brought to light, then eliminated.

- Provide leadership training for people in poverty who want to serve on boards.

Learn more: Read *Bridges to Sustainable Communities,* Philip E. DeVol, 2010.

Bridges Out of Poverty Training Supplement

3. Theory of Change

How things are now: Problem-solving programs of any sort (workforce development, behavioral, emotional, health) require change from individuals. Change is hard, especially for those who are overwhelmed by instability and a lack of resources. Experience tells us that there are few poverty programs that are comprehensive and even fewer that share their *theories of change* with their subjects.

To escape the tyranny of the moment we need:

- A safe place to talk
- Time for dialogue
- Detachment and objectivity
- New information and education
- Thinking and analysis
- Plans and procedural steps
- A support team

"Abstract"

"Concrete"

My Life Now

"Concrete"

P	L	A	N	S

Procedural Steps:

_____

_____

_____

Source: Philip E. DeVol, *Facilitator Notes for Getting Ahead in a Just-Gettin'-By World,* 2013.

Core ideas: Those who manage Bridges initiatives must be experts in facilitating change because we ask for change at four levels: individual, institutional, community, and policy. Living in unstable environments will force people to spend time, social capital, and mental bandwidth to fix problems with cars, childcare, housing, safety, and food. Using reactive problem-solving skills and relationships, they fix problems on the fly over and over again, only to maintain themselves in poverty.

An institution or community that becomes under-resourced may lose sight of the long view and may attempt to solve problems by cutting staff, shifting costs to employees, cutting professional development costs, selling off assets, dropping research and development activities, failing to maintain infrastructure, cutting services, and increasing fees in order to survive. Leaders caught in the tyranny of the moment, or "short-termism," tend to try to solve their problems using the same thinking and solutions again and again.

Getting Ahead investigators are able to use the theory of change even when living in chaos by making a conscious choice to think in the abstract and take the long view. It helps to be in a safe place, with people who share a common language and have sufficient time to devote to the process. To break out of the tyranny of the moment one must go to the abstract, defined by the terms in the "abstract" space. Through detachment and objectivity a person can think, do an analysis that leads to finding new information, make plans, and take procedural steps that will lead to a new future story.

Context: The theory of change laid out in the *Getting Ahead* workbook puts all the cards on the table so that the Getting Ahead investigator can choose to use the change model—or not. It turns out that the Getting Ahead Theory of Change works for institutions and communities too. When they become unstable and under-resourced, they too tend to fall into the tyranny of the moment and their leaders typically seek out immediate, short-term solutions when what they need is a way to break out of the tyranny of the moment.

How to use the tool

- Identify the tyranny of the moment for yourself and others.

- Find a safe place and safe people where you can find the mental bandwidth to think, to be in the abstract.

- Investigate new information.

- Think outside the box or bubble that is formed by a concrete environment.

- Guard against predators who take advantage of chaos.

- Recognize that people in institutions and communities also can get trapped in the tyranny of the moment.

Learn more: Read *Facilitator Notes for Getting Ahead in a Just-Gettin'-By World,* Philip E. DeVol, 2013.

Excerpted from Revised Edition of *Bridges to Sustainable Communities* by P. E. DeVol (2015). Published by aha! Process, Inc.

Bridges Out of Poverty Training Supplement

4. Three Classes at the Table

How things are now: People in poverty are very rarely at the planning and decision-making tables, even when poverty is the issue. The middle class and wealthy have normalized their role as decision makers so thoroughly that invariably they default to taking charge automatically. This entrenched rankism is sometimes seen even in Bridges initiatives.

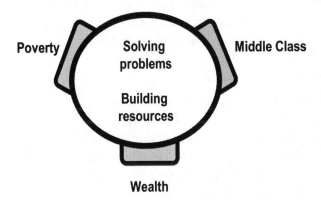

Developed by Terie Dreussi-Smith,
Jodi R. Pfarr, and Philip E. DeVol

Context: People in poverty have information that is vital to planning. They have concrete knowledge of the environment of poverty, the barriers that they encounter when they navigate the systems set up by institutions, and the barriers to upward mobility that exist in the community.

Core ideas: Organizers seek out, invite, and listen to people in poverty. Room must be made at decision-making tables; work, decisions, and leadership must be shared. Everyone is viewed as a problem solver and a co-creator, sometimes playing the role of a coach, sometimes of a challenger. Images of "teaching a man to fish," or "giving someone a hand up" represent the hierarchical structures of class. A more fitting image would be "working shoulder to shoulder." Mike Saccocio of City Mission in Schenectady tells of the day that he was traveling with a Getting Ahead graduate to present to two New York Supreme Court judges when he realized that the roles had reversed: She was the leader, and his role was to drive her there.

Everyone around the table will benefit from examining their own experiences with class structures. And, if need be, recognize that they may have normalized and benefited from their societal status. Becoming conscious of rank and rankism can help people build healthy authentic relationships.

How to use the tool

- Utilize Getting Ahead as an engagement tool. Begin engaging investigators when deciding when and where to conduct the classes. Share the work of making it a successful learning experience. Plan the graduation together and design the follow-up programs and problem-solving strategies together.

- The percentage of people from poverty at the planning table should be at least 25%.

- Provide to the people from poverty the same opportunities that you offer to anyone else to attend leadership courses, board trainings, and national conferences.

Read *From Vision to Action,* Bonnie Bazata et al., 2013, and *The Power of TED—The Empowerment Dynamic,* David Emerald, 2005.

---

5. Community at Risk

How things are now: The number of cities and counties that qualify as distressed is growing; middle-class stability has been shaken; the median household income has been stagnant since the late '70s; the working class is slipping into situational poverty, using safety-net resources to stay above water; and upward mobility has stalled out for most U.S. residents.

Is Your Community at Risk?
Indicators of Distress

(please check those that apply)

☐ Population loss

☐ Middle-class flight

☐ Young-adult children leave the community and don't come back

☐ Lost manufacturing

☐ Tax delinquencies/foreclosures

☐ More temporary and part-time jobs

☐ Rising food insecurity

☐ Low-income housing costs above 30% of income

☐ Growing number of payday lending, cash advance, pawn shops, and lease/purchase outlets

☐ Free and reduced lunch rates rising

☐ Number and value of business loans are declining

☐ Investment in infrastructure is declining

☐ Fiscal difficulties for city or county

☐ City or county hiring freezes or layoffs

☐ Deteriorating Main Street

Source: Philip E. DeVol, *Bridges to Sustainable Communities*, 2010, and *Getting Ahead in Just-Gettin'-By World*, 2013, Module 8.

Context: Communities that use the Bridges constructs recognize that to address poverty effectively we must engage the whole community. This thinking tool is used to bring the distress level of the community to light.

Core ideas: Getting Ahead investigators begin their work by naming the problems they face. This relevant and sometimes painful information acts as a motivator. It is used to create a discrepancy between what is and what could be—a future story. Bridges collaboratives can do the same by naming and facing the problems in a community.

How to use the tool

▪ This list of risk factors in this thinking tool is to be used to spark conversation and investigation. The community bank in Martinsville, Indiana, recognized the connection between distress factors in the community and poverty and was the catalyst for Bridges in its community and beyond.

▪ Utilize information generated by Getting Ahead investigators during the class: the Mental Models of Poverty, Community Assessment, and the Mental Model of Community Prosperity.

▪ Use Module 8 of Getting Ahead to assess the community.

Learn more: Read *Bridges to Sustainable Communities*, Philip E. DeVol, 2010.

6. Bridges Steering Committees

How things are now: There are many things that make it difficult for a community to collaborate. Here's a short list: silos and funding streams that support them, competing agendas/problems/initiatives, partners that come and go as leaders change jobs, short-term planning and goals, differing perceptions regarding the problems, and a lack of common language and metrics.

Core ideas: It is in communities where we can have the greatest impact. It is where we have connections, local knowledge, influence, and, above all, a reason to act. It is, after all, where we live. This tool is descriptive, not prescriptive. It helps conceptualize the work of a Bridges Steering Committee.

How to use the tool

- Communities find their own names for the groups they form—e.g., Marion Matters or Stillwater Cares.

- The "coordination" ring represents the work done by the institution or collaboratives that act in the role of catalyst, sponsor, administrative, and fiscal agent. In some communities the coordination role is shared by two or more organizations according to who the fiscal agent is for a grant or by sharing supportive services. Some communities, such as St. Joseph County (Indiana) Bridges Out of Poverty Initiative, formed a nonprofit that has paid staff, interns, AmeriCorps personnel, and volunteers managing the work under a board of directors. The membership is made up of 40-plus organizations.

- The "membership strategies" ring names some of the actions taken by organizations that are embedding Bridges concepts in their work.

DEVELOPING A BRIDGES COMMUNITY
Purpose and Function of a BRIDGES STEERING COMMITTEE

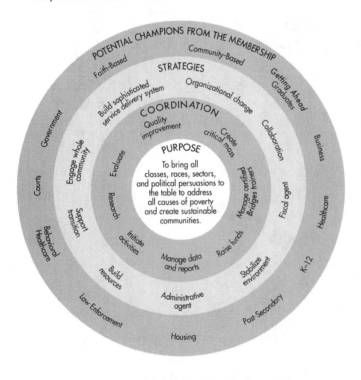

Source: Philip E. DeVol, *Bridges to Sustainable Communities*, 2010.

- Communities will often generate champions who use Bridges so successfully that other organizations in the community and beyond seek them out as models.

- The "thinking tools" are designed to enhance the work of Bridges Steering Committees.

Learn more: Read *Bridges to Sustainable Communities,* Philip E. DeVol, 2010, Chapters 3, 5 (which contains the chart above), and 6.

Context: Bridges provides a common language, core constructs, and tools that will help overcome the barriers listed above. Because poverty impacts all sectors (schools, health, criminal justice, employment, and so on), it is possible for every sector to achieve its goals while participating in a collaborative. In addition, Bridges is not a program, so its concepts can support other national or sector initiatives, such as Opportunity Nation, Healthy Communities, or Strive. In that sense Bridges is an additive that can enhance any initiative.

Excerpted from Revised Edition of *Bridges to Sustainable Communities* by P. E. DeVol (2015). Published by aha! Process, Inc.

7. Community Sustainability Grid

How things are now: As long as our communities (and nation) are confused about the causes of poverty, our strategies to address poverty will be confused. We will be subject to the "either/or" thinking promoted by talk radio, newspapers, cable television, magazines, and think tanks with political agendas. This environment makes it difficult to hold a true dialogue about the problems and to take meaningful action at the community and national level.

by individual choices and behaviors and political/economic structures and everything in between, such as community conditions and exploitation.

How to use the tool

- Identify issues to work on by listening to Getting Ahead graduates. They have the most relevant information on the barriers.

- Use the form to address one barrier or problem at a time.

Community Sustainability Grid A Comprehensive Planning Tool for Bridges Steering Committees				
Name the Barrier:	Individual Behavior	Human and Social Capital in the Community	Exploitation	Political/Economic Structures
Individual Action				
Organizational Action				
Community Action				
Policy				

Address All Causes of Poverty

Source: Philip E. DeVol, *Getting Ahead in a Just-Gettin'-By World,* 2013.

Context: The Community Sustainability Grid is based on the Research Continuum that organizes research topics into four clusters: individual choice and behavior, conditions in the community, exploitation, and political/economic structures. The grid is designed to help a Bridges initiative address all the causes.

Core ideas: There is good research in all four clusters. This means that Bridges initiatives can offer their communities a "both/and" approach to poverty that will attract people from all political persuasions. In other words, poverty is caused both

- Name the barrier in the top left-hand cell in the table.

- Be as thorough as possible when brainstorming and selecting solutions one row at a time.

- Name the specific solution or action step, as well as the responsible person or organization.

Learn more: For an example of a grid that has been filled in, go to the *Getting Ahead* workbook, 2013, pages 220–224.

Excerpted from Revised Edition of *Bridges to Sustainable Communities* by P. E. DeVol (2015). Published by aha! Process, Inc.

8. Bridges Continuum

How things are now: In our communities today most people are looking to someone else to solve the poverty problem. We tend to look first to the individuals in poverty and the organizations that encounter and serve them ("If only __(fill in the blank)__ would __(fill in the blank)__ then __(fill in the blank)__"). Some communities recognize the connection between high poverty rates and community sustainability more quickly than others. The tipping point for some of the more stable communities is when the free- and reduced-lunch rate climbs above 40%. For more distressed communities, however, 40% would be considered an unrealistic goal.

Core ideas: Rather than waiting on federal or state policies to change Bridges initiatives, capitalize on local connections and influence to take action. This tool features these concepts:

- Poverty can be addressed at every stage of life.

- Almost every sector can participate in stabilizing the environment and building resources.

- Community metrics must be identified to set reasonable goals and to serve the purpose of each organization.

THE BRIDGES CONTINUUM
A Comprehensive Planning Tool for Bridges Steering Committees

	Preconception to 6	K–12	Post-Secondary	Workforce Placement	Job Retention	Self-Sufficient Wage	Seniors	Wellness	Community Prosperity
Metrics									
Fallout Costs									
Bridges Strategies									
Responsible for Action									

Source: Philip E. DeVol, *Facilitator Notes for Getting Ahead in a Just-Gettin'-By World,* 2013.

Context: Bridges Communities are the exception to this. Instead of looking to others to address poverty, they take responsibility across multiple sectors. The growth of Bridges initiatives tends to move organically from one or two organizations that use Bridges to the collective realization that collaboration will be more effective and cost-efficient.

- Some people are drawn to Bridges by their hearts, others by their heads. Those drawn by their heads need to see numbers. Poverty is costly; it's not a good economic model.

- Identify the solutions offered by aha! Process and the Bridges Community of Practice.

- Successful approaches in one sector can often be adapted to improve outcomes in another sector. For example, employers have created strategies to improve retention rates. These strategies can then be adapted and used by colleges and universities to improve their graduation rates of under-resourced students.

- This tool illustrates how most organizations can be responsible for doing something to address poverty.

- Bridges can prevent poverty, alleviate suffering, and support people in transition.

How to use the tool

- Share this tool at all trainings; it will help people see how they can fit into the Bridges work.

- Attract people in all sectors.

- Illustrate what each sector can do and how it will benefit by joining the initiative.

- Illustrate the need for collaboration.

- Create a local version of this table.

Learn more: Read *Bridges to Sustainable Communities,* Philip E. DeVol, 2010, and *Facilitator Notes for Getting Ahead in a Just-Gettin'-By World,* Philip E. DeVol, 2013.

9. 'Getting By' Resources vs. 'Getting Ahead' Resources

How things are now: How poverty is defined points to what the solution is expected to be. So in the U.S. the definition is based on income, so the solution must be to increase one's income. This simplistic definition of poverty cannot address the complex causes of poverty, the lack of social coherence, or the balance between a safety net and opportunities for upward mobility. The current approach has devolved into cliff effects that destabilize people just when they most need stability. And many programs have fallen into a pattern of providing people with just enough resources to maintain them in poverty, including individuals who have one or more minimum-wage jobs.

Core ideas: Distinguishing between "getting by" resources and "getting ahead" resources can be difficult. For example, one woman had to choose between taking a better-paying job and losing her subsidized housing. The subsidized housing, which provided much-needed stability, was a disincentive for change. She said, "It's scary to step from a shaky safety net to a shaky ladder. Who knows if the job will be there next year?"

Institutions and funders need to determine if they are merely bringing resources to people on the one hand or helping them build resources on the other. All of these decisions come together as a piece that

	Financial	Emotional	Mental	Spiritual	Physical	Support Systems	Relationships/ Role Models	Knowledge of Hidden Rules	Integrity and Trust	Motivation and Persistence	Formal Register
'Getting By' Resources											
'Getting Ahead' Resources											

Adapted from J. Pfarr Consulting

Context: In Bridges, poverty is defined as the extent to which individuals, institutions, and communities do without resources. That concept gives everyone something to do about poverty: build resources. This tool deepens our understanding of the 11 resources by giving communities a way to think and talk about the balance between a safety net and a support system for making the transition out of poverty.

determines whether or not someone can make the climb out of poverty. Communities that offer Getting Ahead must make a commitment to support people in poverty during that long, hard climb.

Excerpted from Revised Edition of *Bridges to Sustainable Communities* by P. E. DeVol (2015). Published by aha! Process, Inc.

How to use the tool

- Individuals analyze their resources during Getting Ahead classes.

- Institutions can analyze the resources they provide. St. Vincent de Paul, a national faith-based organization that has a long history of working directly with the poor, is using this tool to rebalance its approach.

- Community collaboratives can use the tool to review resource utilization and opportunities. A number of food banks are thinking how they can "shorten the line" by addressing root causes of food insecurity.

- Funders are particularly interested in initiative-based approaches rather than needs-based funding. They have the flexibility to change how funding is allocated in ways that most fixed federal and state programs don't.

- Use this tool to open a discussion on funding patterns. Much of the funding for poverty is designed to help people manage poverty. Those organizations often resist initiative-based funding because it threatens their funding stream and their staff. Finding innovative ways to shift some funds to support people who are moving out of poverty is a current debate. This thinking tool feeds that conversation at the local, state, and national levels.

Excerpted from Revised Edition of *Bridges to Sustainable Communities* by P. E. DeVol (2015). Published by aha! Process, Inc.

Bridges Out of Poverty Training Supplement

10. Methodology: Innovation

How things are now: Top-down models of *knowledge transfer* often prescribe programs that require compliance. They are not always open to innovation and are less likely to be sustainable because local adopters have taken little ownership of the concepts.

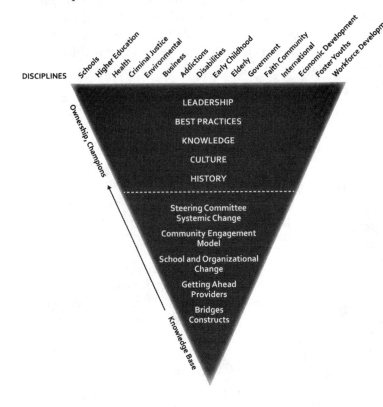

DISCIPLINES
Schools, Higher Education, Health, Criminal Justice, Environmental, Business, Addictions, Disabilities, Early Childhood, Elderly, Government, Faith Community, International, Economic Development, Foster Youths, Workforce Development

Ownership, Champions

LEADERSHIP
BEST PRACTICES
KNOWLEDGE
CULTURE
HISTORY

Steering Committee
Systemic Change

Community Engagement
Model

School and Organizational
Change

Getting Ahead
Providers

Bridges
Constructs

Knowledge Base

Source: aha! Process, "Platform for Economic Justice," 2007.

Context: As noted, Bridges is not a program but a set of shared constructs that can be applied in many ways. These concepts, books, and trainings come from Bridges consultants and aha! Process, Inc. People are first attracted to the concepts. But they also are attracted to the Bridges methodology, which is that individuals, institutions, and communities are encouraged to "own" the concepts, to see themselves as co-creators, and to invent new programs and strategies.

Core ideas: In Bridges everyone, starting with people in poverty, is viewed as problem solvers. The co-creator concept includes those around the coffeepot at particular agencies, people in the community who are also using Bridges, people from particular sectors, Bridges sites from around the country, and Bridges consultants. This natural learning process has generated a network of Bridges sites out of which has come Advancing Bridges, Inc., an independent non-profit with the mission of building the Bridges movement.

How to use the tool

- Bridges provides the basic concepts and some programs that appear under the dotted line in the mental model above.
- Those who apply the concepts naturally take into account the history, culture, knowledge base, leadership, and best practices of their organization, community, or discipline. Judge Carol Robb, Columbiana County (Ohio) Municipal Court, made nine policy changes in her court that not only saved the county money but helped stabilize the lives of the offenders. The simplest change was to switch from specific appointment times for offenders to see the probation officer to setting a day and time by which the meeting with the probation officer must take place. This saved the county the cost of issuing bench warrants and stabilized the lives of offenders by not needing to send them to jail. Several courts in Ohio and beyond have also adopted this strategy.
- The solutions that arise from this methodology will then be relevant and sustainable. Adopting this thinking tool can open the door to the expansion of Bridges into many more disciplines or sectors.

Learn more: Read article: "What Makes Getting Ahead and Bridges Work?" Philip E. DeVol, n.d.

Excerpted from Revised Edition of *Bridges to Sustainable Communities* by P. E. DeVol (2015). Published by aha! Process, Inc.

11. Cycle of Innovation: Knowledge and Technology

How things are now: Bridges sites may be creating new solutions and not have the intention or capacity to share their new ideas with others. During the process of building a Bridges initiative, individuals, organizations, and communities move along the learning continuum from novice to expert. In a learning community of so many sites, sectors, and communities, movement from novice, beginner, competent, proficient, and expert is uneven. In addition, the Bridges Community of Practice has not been formalized.

Context: aha! Process provides books, trainings, and consulting. In addition, it offers the learning community quarterly teleconferences for various sectors; websites; blogs; webinars; newsletters; an annual conference; and *From Vision to Action,* a publication of best practices. As the knowledge base grows, so does the demand for a systemic approach to managing and spreading new information.

Core ideas: Breakthrough innovations can occur at any time. When they do, technology can be used to spread the information from individuals to institutions and communities. Evidence must be collected and reported to ensure growth. The marriage of innovations and technology seems self-evident when looking at the rapid growth of new products in the digital world, but for people working on poverty issues, it is more remote. A structure and technology tools are needed to capture and share new, sometimes brilliant, ideas.

How to use the tool

- This thinking tool is designed to illustrate the random way in which brilliant breakthroughs can occur and how technology can move the new information from the individual to the community.

- It's also designed to help communities establish an intention to participate in the cycle of innovation to become champion sites that others seek out. Cascade Engineering, a plastics firm in Michigan, was the first Bridges champion by creating an approach that improved its retention rate of under-resourced workers dramatically. Cascade's breakthrough has led to more breakthroughs in the business sector.

**Cycle of Innovation
Knowledge and Technology
Ever Open to the Next Breakthrough Idea**

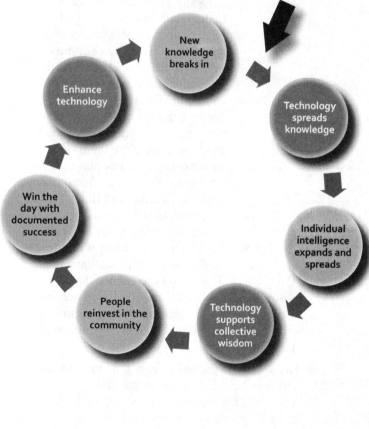

Developed by Jodi R. Pfarr

- Bridges sites need to begin with the end in mind—that is to say, decide on a data-gathering evaluation tool and invest in technology.

- Establish a historian—someone to document the progress, identify the innovations and Bridges concepts that sparked them, maintain a database of those trained in Bridges and Getting Ahead, and celebrate the results.

- Individual organizations can investigate the use of MPOWR's cloud-based data management and reporting system. The full package collects data on the development of the 11 resources for Getting Ahead graduates, 15 life areas, individual case planning, and case management. MPOWR also has a Getting Ahead Module that provides data about development of the 11 resources.

- Community collaboratives can investigate the use of MPOWR across several organizations, thus creating a single plan for GA grads or clients rather than having a plan at every organization. This provides common outcomes for all collaborative members—and access to national data from Bridges sites.

Learn more: Read *The Wisdom of Crowds,* James Surowiecki, 2005.

12. Bridges Communities of Practice Model

How things are now: Even though learning communities are a natural and organic way of learning, they are difficult to support when the members are from many states and sectors—and seven countries! In addition, champion sites can be overwhelmed by the number of calls they field from new Bridges sites. While the basic technology for a web-based learning community exists, the maintenance of this learning and knowledge transfer model is still relatively new and does not include all sites.

Context: aha! Process conducts webinars, publishes books, issues newsletters, and hosts an annual conference.

In 2013 the nonprofit organization Advancing Bridges was formed to promote and support the Bridges movement, adding another link in the learning community.

Core ideas: Members of the Bridges Community of Practice include individual Bridges sites, city or countywide Bridges collaboratives, statewide Bridges initiatives, and sector communities of practice (criminal justice, employers, post-secondary, Getting Ahead, health/healthcare, etc.). The lines that link the communities of practice are both formal and informal. The knowledge base is expanding and becoming more effective at sharing information and supporting new initiatives.

How to use the tool

- Be intentional about participating in the Bridges Community of Practice.

- Assign board members to attend community of practice teleconferences so they can report back on the latest information coming from such sectors as criminal justice, post-secondary, health/healthcare, re-entry, and employer/workforce.

- Participate in multiple-site program development.

- Share best practices and outcomes through publications and websites, as well as at national conferences.

Bridges Communities of Practice Model

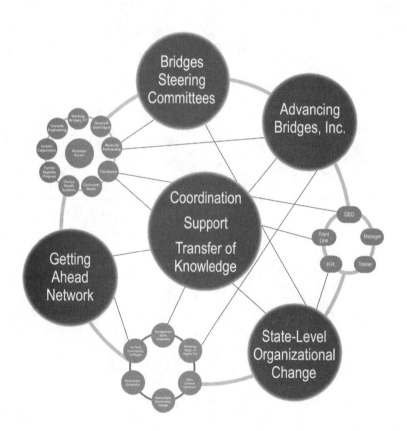

Developed by Terie Dreussi-Smith, Jodi R. Pfarr, and Philip E. DeVol

Learn more: Read *Cultivating Communities of Practice: A Guide to Managing Knowledge,* Etienne Wenger, Richard McDermott, & William M. Snyder, 2002.

Excerpted from Revised Edition of *Bridges to Sustainable Communities* by P. E. DeVol (2015). Published by aha! Process, Inc.

Conclusion

Utilizing these 12 thinking tools is a form of participatory action research. People involved in Bridges initiatives learn through their investigations and the innovative ideas they put into action, using the growth of their knowledge to feed the cycle of learning. This means that individuals, organizations, and communities can benefit by applying Bridges concepts even while they are contributing to the next cycle of learning and a deeper level of impact.

Bridges has been called a movement because it grows naturally, as if on its own. People want to join because they can see that good things will happen. It is a social movement that inspires people to work together and in so doing build social capital; it is an economic movement because its purpose is to bring stability, security, and a higher quality of life. Bridges isn't a political movement, even though it must eventually influence policymakers.

Political/economic promoters offer "narratives" or a story line that presents their explanation of the past and their version of what the future might be and pit one group against another. The Bridges narrative is free of, and broader than, existing narratives because it isn't bound by the absolutes of competing economic and political ideologies. It's a safe place in the center of the community where sensible, non-partisan dialogue guides action.

Two recent studies confirm that there is middle ground where reasonable people can meet to solve community problems. The studies point to what we in Bridges have already found to be true; conservatives and progressives largely agree on many key aspects about poverty. There are Bridges sites in communities known to be very conservative and in communities that are regarded as very progressive or liberal. And we know they are all using Bridges concepts to take action on the serious problems of poverty and community sustainability.

The McClatchy-Marist National Poll survey of 1,197 adults was conducted between February 4 and 9, 2014. The other recent poll was designed and conducted by the Half in Ten Campaign and the Center for American Progress; it was released in January 2014.

The McClatchy-Marist poll shows that Democrats, Independents, and Republicans largely agreed that it takes even more effort to get ahead in the United States these days than in previous generations. Their responses to the question about "more effort":

Strong Democrats	85%
Soft Democrats	77%
Just Independents	82%
Soft Republicans	77%
Strong Republicans	82%

To the question, "In this country right now, do you think people who work hard have a good chance of improving their standard of living" or "still have a hard time maintaining their standard of living," people from all three groups largely agreed that "people still have a hard time maintaining their standard of living."

Strong Democrats	72%
Soft Democrats	72%
Just Independents	75%
Soft Republicans	65%
Strong Republicans	58%

The findings from "50 Years After LBJ's War on Poverty: A Study of American Attitudes About Work, Economic Opportunity, and the Social Safety Net" done by the Center for American Progress, in cooperation with the Half in Ten Campaign, address the attitudes people have about individuals in poverty.

Excerpted from Revised Edition of *Bridges to Sustainable Communities* by P. E. DeVol (2015). Published by aha! Process, Inc.

To the question, "Do you agree or disagree: 'Most people living in poverty are decent people who are working hard to make ends meet in a difficult economy'?" Most people agreed with the statement.

Millennials	82%
African Americans	92%
Latinos	82%
White liberals/progressives	92%
White moderates	76%
White conservatives/libertarians	66%

To the question, "Do you agree or disagree: 'The primary reason so many people are living in poverty today is that our economy is failing to produce enough jobs that pay decent wages'?" Most people agreed with the statement:

Millennials	77%
African Americans	78%
Latinos	80%
White liberals/progressives	79%
White moderates	80%
White conservatives/libertarians	76%

There is every reason for Bridges Communities to take hope and energy from these findings, as well as from their own experience working with people across class and political lines. It is increasingly urgent that we become ever more effective because, frankly, it isn't likely that the global economy will suddenly change course and start promoting stable workplace environments and more opportunities to build resources. The healthiest response in these difficult times is to work in our own communities, document our success, and create a narrative—a future story—that others also can benefit from and put into practice.

Excerpted from Revised Edition of *Bridges to Sustainable Communities* by P. E. DeVol (2015). Published by aha! Process, Inc.

Bridges Out of Poverty Training Supplement

Glossary

Bridges Out of Poverty: the title of the book that has been shortened to "Bridges" when referring to concepts, initiatives, and communities.

Bridges Community: a place where there is a Bridges Steering Committee.

Bridges initiative: a program or approach that is based on Bridges and conducted by a single organization or collaborative.

Bridges Steering Committee: the people from various organizations who are using Bridges concepts and meet regularly to collaborate and expand the work.

Common language: shared information on environments of class, causes of poverty, hidden rules of class, language issues, resources, etc.

Community of Practice: a structured approach for people within a discipline or movement who intend to document and improve their practices.

Getting Ahead: referring to the workbook and accompanying facilitator notes, *Getting Ahead in a Just-Gettin'-By World.*

Getting Ahead: referring to the program in which people from poverty graduate after taking a 12-week course.

Hidden rules: the unspoken cues and habits of a group that arise from their environment.

Learning community: a group that learns together with activities and intention but not as a formal Community of Practice.

Mental models: stories, metaphors, parables, videos, and two-dimensional drawings that represent complex abstract ideas. Also an internal picture or world view.

MPOWR: a cloud-based data collection and evaluation tool provided by SupplyCore, Inc.

Resources: Ruby Payne's definition of poverty is "the extent to which an individual does without resources": financial, mental, social/support systems, emotional, physical, spiritual, language/formal register, motivation and persistence, integrity and trust, relationships/role models, knowledge of hidden rules.

Excerpted from Revised Edition of *Bridges to Sustainable Communities* by P. E. DeVol (2015). Published by aha! Process, Inc.

Bibliography—Suggested Reading

aha! Process. (2007). A platform for economic justice. Retrieved from http://www.ahaprocess.com/wp-content/uploads/2013/09/Platform-for-Economic-Justice.pdf

Bazata, B., Saccocio, M., Varian, N., Clark-Thomas, B., Nicholson, R. H., Taylor, C., … Stoddard, L. (2013). *From vision to action: Best practices to reduce the impact of poverty in communities, education, healthcare, and more.* Highlands, TX: aha! Process.

Berne, E. (1996). *Games people play.* New York, NY: Ballantine Books.

Brouwer, S. (1998). *Sharing the pie: A citizen's guide to wealth and power in America.* New York, NY: Henry Holt.

Covey, S. R. (1989). *The seven habits of highly effective people: Powerful lessons in personal change.* New York, NY: Simon & Schuster.

de Soto, H. (2000). *The mystery of capital: Why capitalism triumphs in the West and fails everywhere else.* New York, NY: Basic Books.

DeVol, P. E. (n.d.). What makes Bridges and Getting Ahead work for individuals, institutions, and communities. Retrieved from http://www.ahaprocess.com/wp-content/uploads/2013/11/GA-What-Makes-Bridges-GA-Work.pdf

DeVol, P. E. (2006). *Getting ahead in a just-gettin'-by world* (2nd rev. ed.). Highlands, TX: aha! Process.

DeVol, P. E. (2010). *Bridges to sustainable communities: A systemwide, cradle-to-grave approach to ending poverty in America.* Highlands, TX: aha! Process.

DeVol, P. E. (2013). *Facilitator notes for getting ahead in a just-gettin'-by world* (3rd rev. ed.). Highlands, TX: aha! Process.

DeVol, P. E. (2015). *Getting ahead in a just-gettin'-by world* (3rd rev. ed.). Highlands, TX: aha! Process.

Emerald, D. (2005). *The power of TED—The empowerment dynamic.* Bainbridge Island, WA: Polaris.

Farson, R. (1997). *Management of the absurd: Paradoxes in leadership.* New York, NY: Touchstone.

Freedman, J., & Combs, G. (1996) *Narrative therapy: The social construction of preferred realities.* New York, NY: W. W. Norton.

Galeano, E. (1998). *Upside down: A primer for the looking-glass world.* New York, NY: Metropolitan Books.

Gladwell, M. (2000). *The tipping point: How little things can make a big difference.* Boston, MA: Little, Brown.

Goleman, D. (1995). *Emotional intelligence.* New York, NY: Bantam Books.

Harrison, L. E., & Huntington, S. P. (Eds.). (2000). *Culture matters: How values shape human progress.* New York, NY: Basic Books.

Hart, B., & Risley, T. R. (1995). *Meaningful differences in the everyday experience of young American children.* Baltimore, MD: Paul H. Brookes.

Hawkins, P., Lovins, A., & Lovins, L. H. (1999). *Natural capitalism: Creating the next industrial revolution.* Boston, MA: Little, Brown.

hooks, b. (2000). *Where we stand: Class matters.* New York, NY: Routledge.

Kelly, M. (2001). *The divine right of capital: Dethroning the corporate aristocracy.* San Francisco, CA: Berrett-Koehler.

Lareau, A. (2003). *Unequal childhoods: Class, race, and family life.* Berkeley, CA: University of California Press.

Levine, M. (2002). *A mind at a time.* New York, NY: Simon and Schuster.

Lind, M. (2004). Are we still a middle-class nation? *The Atlantic, 293*(1), pp. 120–128.

Mattaini, M. A. (1993). *More than a thousand words: Graphics for clinical practice.* Washington, DC: NASW Press.

Miller, W. R., & Rollnick, S. (2002). *Motivational interviewing: Preparing people for change* (2nd ed.). New York, NY: Guilford Press.

O'Connor, A. (2001). *Poverty knowledge: Social science, social policy, and the poor in twentieth-century U.S. history.* Princeton, NJ: Princeton University Press.

Oshry, B. (1996). *Seeing systems: Unlocking the mysteries of organizational life.* San Francisco, CA: Berrett-Koehler.

Payne, R. K. (2013). *A framework for understanding poverty* (5th rev. ed.). Highlands, TX: aha! Process.

Pfarr, J. R. (2013). *Tactical communication: Mastering effective interactions with citizens from diverse economic backgrounds* (First responder ed.). Highlands, TX: aha! Process.

Putnam, R. D. (2000). *Bowling alone: The collapse and revival of American community.* New York, NY: Simon and Schuster.

Sapolsky, R. M. (2004). *Why zebras don't get ulcers: An updated guide to stress, stress-related diseases, and coping.* New York, NY: W. H. Freeman.

Schwartz, P. (1996). *The art of the long view: Planning for the future in an uncertain world.* New York, NY: Currency Doubleday.

Senge, P. M. (1994). *The fifth discipline: The art and practice of the learning organization.* New York, NY: Currency Doubleday.

Sharron, H., & Coulter, M. (2004). *Changing children's minds: Feuerstein's revolution in the teaching of intelligence* (4th ed.). Highlands, TX: aha! Process.

Shipler, D. K. (2004). *The working poor: Invisible in America.* New York, NY: Alfred A. Knopf.

Stewart, T. A. (1997). *Intellectual capital: The new wealth of organizations.* New York, NY: Currency Doubleday.

Stosny, S. (2003). *The powerful self.* Silver Spring, MD: BookSurge.

Surowiecki, J. (2005). *The wisdom of crowds.* New York, NY: Anchor Books.

Taylor-Ide, D., & Taylor C. E. (2002). *Just and lasting change: When communities own their futures.* Baltimore, MD: Johns Hopkins University Press.

United States Census Bureau. (2012). American community survey [Data file]. Retrieved from https://www.census.gov/programs-surveys/acs/data.html/

United States Department of Housing and Urban Development. (2000, March). Rental housing assistance—The worsening crisis: A report to Congress on worst case housing needs. Retrieved from https://www.huduser.gov/portal//publications/pdf/HUD-11029-2.pdf

United States Department of Housing and Urban Development. (2012). The 2012 point-in-time estimates of homelessness: Volume I of the 2012 annual homeless assessment report. Retrieved from https://www.hudexchange.info/resources/documents/2012AHAR_PITestimates.pdf

United States Department of Housing and Urban Development. (2015, April). Worst case housing needs: 2015 report to Congress. Retrieved from https://www.huduser.gov/portal/Publications/pdf/WorstCaseNeeds_2015.pdf

Vella, J. (2002). *Learning to listen, learning to teach*: The power of dialogue in educating adults. San Francisco, CA: Jossey-Bass.

Warren, E., & Warren-Tyagi, A. (2003). *The two-income trap: Why middle-class mothers and fathers are going broke.* New York, NY: Basic Books.

Wenger, E., McDermott, R., & Snyder, W. M. (2002). *Cultivating communities of practice.* Brighton, MA: Harvard Business Review Press.

More eye-openers at ... www.ahaprocess.com

- **Visit www.ahaprocess.com for *free resources*: articles, video clips, success stories from practitioners, and read our aha! Moments blog!**

- **Sign up for our latest workshop offerings (many online), including:**
    - Bridges To Health and Healthcare
    - Investigations into Economic Class in America
    - Getting Ahead in a Just-Gettin'-By World
    - Applying Bridges Concepts: Individual, and Institutional
    - Bridges Out of Poverty Trainer Certification
    - Building a Sustainable Community
    - Understanding Class for First Responders

- **Visit www.gettingaheadnetwork.com for more information on community-based models that will work where you live**

- **If you like *Bridges Out of Poverty,* check out these publications:**
    - *How Much of Yourself Do You Own? A process for building your emotional resources* (Payne & Baker-O'Neill)
    - *Getting Ahead While Getting Out: A prisoner reentry model to reduce recidivism through learning, building resources, accountability, and collaboration* (DeVol, Libster, & Wood)
    - *Bridges to Health and Healthcare:* New solutions for improving access and services (Payne, Dreussi-Smith, Shaw, & Young).
    - New Revised Edition of *From Vision to Action: Best Practices to reduce the impact of poverty in communities, education, healthcare, and more (Peer Reviewed articles written by practitioners of the work)*
    - *Investigations into Economic Class in America & Facilitator Notes* (DeVol & Krodel). This is *Getting Ahead* adapted for college students.
    - *Bridges to Sustainable Communities: A Systemwide, Cradle-to-Grave Approach to Ending Poverty in America* (DeVol) for techniques, training, and tips for generating Bridges Communities
    - *Tactical Communication: Mastering Effective Interactions with citizens of diverse backgrounds* (Pfarr)

- **Connect with us on FaceBook, Twitter, Pinterest, and watch our YouTube channel**

    For a complete listing of products, please visit www.ahaprocess.com

Join us on Facebook

www.facebook.com/rubypayne
www.facebook.com/bridgesoutofpoverty
www.facebook.com/ahaprocess
www.facebook.com/CollegeAchievementAlliance

Twitter

www.twitter.com/ahaprocess
#povertychat
#BridgesOutofPoverty

Pinterest

http://www.pinterest.com/ahaprocess/

Subscribe to our YouTube channel

www.youtube.com/ahaprocess

Respond to our blog

www.ahaprocess.com/blog

Download free resources

www.ahaprocess.com